BRAIN
TWISTERS

TEST◇YOUR
INTELLIGENCE

BRAIN
TWISTERS

NORMAN
SULLIVAN

WARD LOCK

A WARD LOCK BOOK

First published in the UK 1992
by Ward Lock
(a Cassell imprint)
Villiers House
41/47 Strand
LONDON
WC2N 5JE

Distributed in the United States
by Sterling Publishing Co., Inc.
387 Park Avenue South, New York, NY 10016-8810

Distributed in Australia
by Capricorn Link (Australia) Pty Ltd
P.O. Box 665, Lane Cove, NSW 2066

British Library Cataloguing in Publication Data
A catalogue record for this book is available from the British Library

ISBN 0 7063 7086 4

Printed and bound in Great Britain by
Cox & Wyman Ltd, Reading, Berks

Contents

Read This First

'Intelligence' virtually defies definition. People either have it or they do not. Perhaps it can be acquired, and it seems likely that it can be inherited, although under the influences of environment and social contacts it may diminish or increase. An inquisitorial frame of mind, coupled with irrepressible keenness to fathom the seemingly unfathomable, may provide fertile ground for its development, although a neglect of mental exercise may choke it before it can germinate.

Intelligence cannot by any means be entirely equated with education, since a comparatively ill-educated person may be very intelligent – if we are assuming that such an attribute is recognizable – even though he or she lacks any depth of knowledge. Nor is it a necessary complement to manual abilities or subjective skills.

If, in an endeavour to pin down the word, we use an arbitrary definition – 'the ability to apply logical reasoning to a subject, even though there is no particular knowledge of, or flair for, that subject' – we are left with the question: what subjects should be used to test comprehensive reasoning in a book such as this, offering as it does, objective and multiple-choice questions, since it is not possible to assess 'motor skills', which call for manual dexterity, or artistic talents?

It is usually considered acceptable to give tests in specific subjects that are sufficiently wide-ranging to give a reasonably all-round assessment of the reader's general understanding – the ability to get to the root of a problem that may never have been encountered in the past, for example, or answering a question that is posed in a form different from that previously met.

These subjects are verbal skills combined with a reasonable vocabulary; skills of numeracy; visual-spatial ability and visual perception, including the recognition of shapes when their positions are changed relative to the viewer; and the ability to reason and deduce logically – that is, to infer facts from a given premise. Deduction may, in fact, be called for in conjunction with any of the above.

A person may be a genius in one subject but fail abysmally in one or all of the others. Therefore, in devising these tests I have ensured that there are an almost equal number of problems in each subject, and the 165 problems are made up as follows: verbal skills – 26 per cent; numerical skills – 33 per cent; spatial discrimination – 21 per cent; and logical reasoning and deduction – 17 per cent. There remain a very small number – 3 per cent – that are based on general knowledge. Despite my previous assertion that knowledge is not equated with intelligence, it is fair to suppose that a certain amount of knowledge is gleaned from day-to-day news and happenings within one's own experience. For that reason I have included a very few questions that call for general, as opposed to specialized, knowledge.

Speed of comprehension may, in itself, be regarded as intelligence. If sufficient time were devoted to most problems, their solutions would probably emerge eventually. For this reason I have set severe time limits for each test. I use the word 'severe' because throughout this book I have tried to balance speed with difficulty. Thus, shorter times have been allowed for the solution of comparatively simple tests. In addition, some problems call for more writing than others, and in all such cases this has been taken into consideration when the time limits were set. Because some people write more slowly than others, time limits have been notionally imposed on the slowest writers.

How to Prepare for The Tests

Assuming that you intend to approach these tests seriously, with the object of comparing your rating with those given at the end of each group, you should – before even glancing at the questions – have the following to hand. Firstly, you should have a clock or a watch from which you should note the time when you start each test so that you finish as soon as the time limit is reached. If you have not finished all the questions, by all means continue to the end of that particular test, but do not include any unfinished problems in your score. Secondly you will need a pen or pencil and some paper so that not only can you write down the answers but also record and keep a note of your score after each test. Some questions will demand more writing than others, although most are answered with a single letter, word or number, and some require the copying of simple grids. Do not use tracing–paper or a pocket calculator; using either of these would put you at an unfair advantage.

How to Check Your Rating

There are three groups of tests, and they are all graduated according to difficulty: Group I is easy, Group II is more difficult and Group III is difficult.

After each test, check your answers against those given on the following pages and make a note of your score. Keep this record until you have completed **all** the tests, when you will be able to check your overall rating.

In addition to checking your answers you should also read the explanations that are included, especially for those questions that you answered wrongly or failed to answer altogether. In this way you will acquire a greater understanding of the reasoning behind the questions and be better prepared to pit your wits against future questions.

Here I would like to offer a word of advice, and this applies not only to the way you should tackle these tests but also to the way in which you should go about tests in other examinations: do not spend too much time on any one particular question if the answer does not come too readily. That time could be better spent on other questions that you find easier. The one question that has – at least temporarily – stumped you may be worth only one point, and during the time you spend on it you could probably answer three or four other questions and gain three, four or even more points.

As you check your results after each test do not be disheartened if you seem to be getting low scores. Not only are some of the problems (whatever the subject) pretty tough, but the time limits have been deliberately imposed to restrict scoring unless ability is accompanied with speed of comprehension.

You may, of course, prefer to regard the tests purely as a diversion to pass the time (constructively, I hope!) without worrying about time limits, scores or ratings, but however you go about them, I hope you will enjoy what follows, even if you don't rate in the genius class!

Now I'll leave you to it. Good luck!

Norman Sullivan

Acknowledgement

I would like to express my deep appreciation to the editor, Lydia Darbyshire, for her painstaking care in preparing this book for publication.

GROUP I
– Easy –

Test 1

Time limit: 20 minutes

1. Which one spoils the frieze?

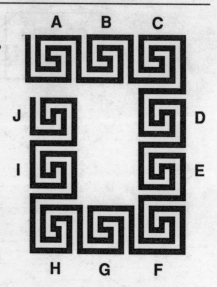

2. Which of the words on the right should go in the brackets?

PHANTOM
MOTTO
OTTOMAN
NAMED
DEMON
NOMINAL
LANYARD

A. RADIO
B. ARYAN
C. ANYWHERE
D. DRAGNET
E. ADROIT
F. ARDENT

(_____)

3. Two different letters can go into the empty space to complete two different words. You must give both words. No proper names allowed.

4. Which row is the odd one out?

A ✕ Ⅿ ╱ ▢ ✳

B ◁ │ ◺ ∧ ⬠

C ⊥ ✛ ⦀ ╲ ⇧

D — ⌞ ◿ Ⅿ ▢

5. How many six-letter words can you make out of:

DECART

15

6. From the example above, decide what goes into the empty bracket below.

$$5\ 1\ 2\ (4\ 2\ 3\ 5\ 1\ 6)\ 6\ 4\ 3$$

$$7\ 8\ 6\ (\qquad\qquad)\ 4\ 1\ 2$$

7. Change HEAD into TAIL in five moves, changing one letter at a time and making genuine words each time.

    HEAD
1. _ _ _ _
2. _ _ _ _
3. _ _ _ _
4. _ _ _ _
5. TAIL

8.　　　　If　$13 \times 3 = 40,$
　　　　　　$12 \times 3 = 35,$
　　　　　　$15 \times 3 = 46$
　　and　$16 \times 3 = 47,$

what does　$17 \times 3 = ?$

9. Taking the initials of these countries in order, what word will result?

10. How many hexagons (six-sided figures) can you find here?

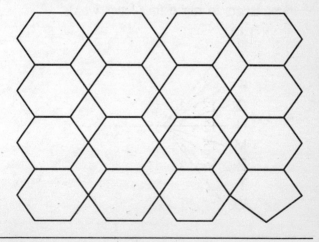

11. Which of the figures at the bottom, A, B or C, should take the place of number 3?

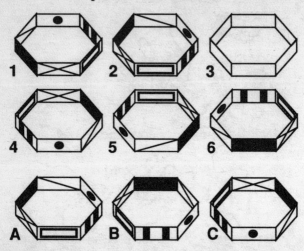

12. What three-letter word can be added to each of these letters to make four-letter words?

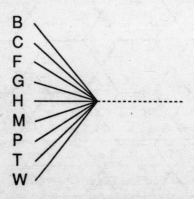

13. Take one letter from each word and rearrange the remaining letters to make flowers.
   A. DISMAY
   B. OPENLY
   C. STORE
   D. STARED
   E. SNAPPY

14. Which letter in the bottom line belongs to the top line?

   A F H Y Z N
   E I K L M X T V W

15. What numbers should there be in the bottom row?

   6 9 4 2
   9 4 2 6
   - - - -

**NOW CHECK YOUR ANSWERS
AND KEEP A NOTE OF YOUR SCORE.**

Answers

1. H **(Score 1 point)**

The centre stroke is shorter.

2. D **(Score 1 point)**

Each word begins with the last three letters of the previous word reversed.

3. T and E **(Score 1 point if both correct)**

The words are TURBAN and URBANE.

4. D **(Score 1 point)**

Apart from D, each row contains one figure with one stroke, one with two strokes, one with three strokes, one with four strokes and one with five strokes. In row D there are two figures with four strokes and none with five strokes.

5. Four words **(Score 1 point if all correct)**

REDACT, CARTED, TRACED, CRATED.

6. 1 6 2 7 8 4 **(Score 1 point)**

The numbers outside the brackets are transposed inside the brackets in the same order as in the top line.

7. 1. HEAR, 2. HEIR, 3. HAIR, 4. HAIL **(Score 1 point. You may score 1 point if you have used other words as long as they are genuine words.)**

8. 52 **(Score 1 point)**

The results are increased by 1 and decreased by 1 alternately: $17 \times 3 = 51 + 1 = 52$

9. STIFFNESS **(Score 1 point)**

The countries are: 1. Sicily – S, 2. Turkey – T, 3. Iceland – I, 4. France – F, 5. Finland – F, 6. Norway – N, 7. England – E, 8. Spain – S, 9. Scotland – S.

10. 21 **(Score 1 point)**

There are 15 small hexagons and 6 large ones. The last shape in the bottom row is a pentagon.

11. B (Score 1 point)

The figure is rotating clockwise.

12. ALL (Score 1 point)

The words are: BALL, CALL, FALL, GALL, HALL, MALL, PALL, TALL, WALL.

13. A. DAISY, B. PEONY, C. ROSE, D. ASTER, E. PANSY (Score 1 point if all correct)

14. K (Score 1 point)

All the letters in the top row consist of three strokes. The only letter in the bottom row that also consists of three strokes is K.

15. 4 2 6 9 (Score 1 point)

The numbers are transposed in the same order as the parts of the man in the top three rows.

REMEMBER TO KEEP A NOTE OF YOUR SCORE.

Notes: No great difficulties. You may not have spotted both the words in Question 3 (mainly because you were trying to beat the time limit). For the same reason, all four words in Question 5 may have eluded you. Questions 6, 7 and 8 were very easy, but Question 9 called for some knowledge of geography. Question 10 probably caught you out; even if you noticed the six large hexagons, you may have overlooked the fact that the last small figure has only five sides. Question 14 called for deduction – as, indeed, did Question 15, although this was much easier.

Time limit: 20 minutes

1.

is to

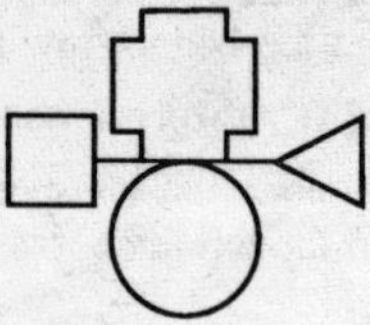

as

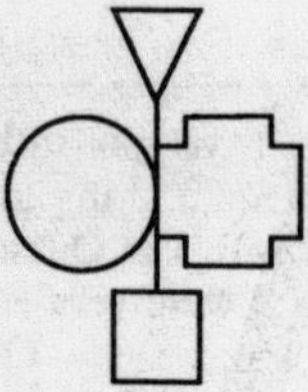

is to ?

A 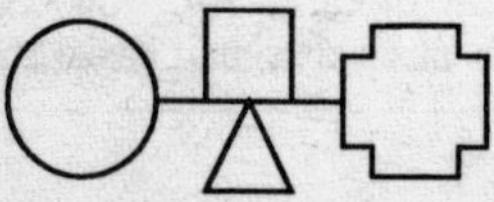 **B**

C 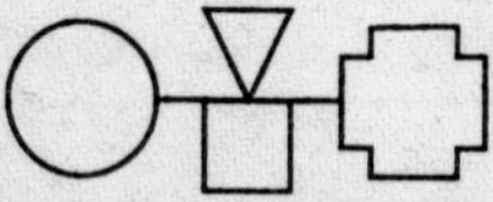 **D**

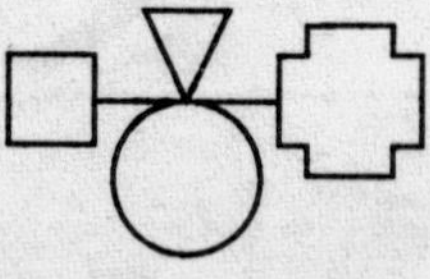

2. Which is the odd one out?

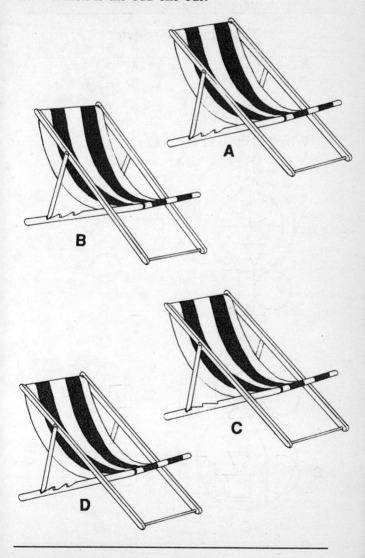

3. Which arithmetical signs should go into the brackets to complete the equations?

A. 5 ( ) 5 ( ) 5 = 2
B. 4 ( ) 4 ( ) 4 = 4
C. 3 ( ) 3 ( ) 3 = 6
D. 2 ( ) 2 ( ) 2 = 8

4. Which is the odd one out?

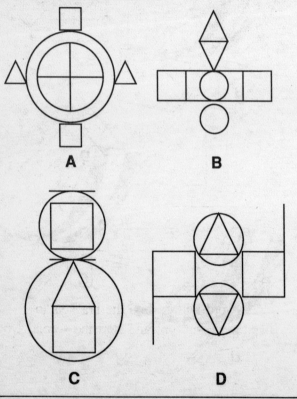

A

B

C

D

5. Which of the shapes below, A, B, C, D or E, is identical to the one above?

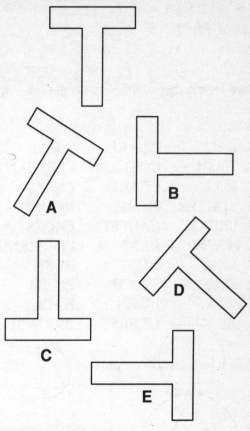

6. What word will go into the brackets to complete the first word and start the second word?

LIME (   ) HAW

7. What number goes into the empty brackets?

    16 (4 2 5 6)
     9 (3 8 1)
    25 (   )

8. Give words that will link with the other three words.

A. BALL	BOARD	SHEEP
B. WASH	COLLAR	ELEPHANT
C. BELL	BEARD	CHIP
D. MATTER	FRIAR	HOUND
E. BREAST	CARPET	CROSS
F. FEVER	RUNNER	PIMPERNEL
G. LEAF	DUST	RUSH
H. SCREEN	BIRCH	PAPER
I. BELT	HORN	BACK
J. OIL	GREEN	BRANCH

9. Which is the odd one out?

    A. TOO PAT
    B. APE
    C. KEEL
    D. PIT RUN
    E. WEEDS
    F. LUMP

10. Which is the odd one out?

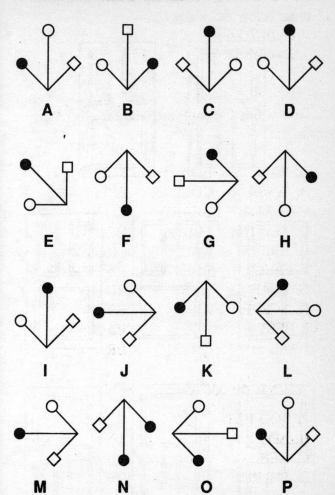

A B C D

E F G H

I J K L

M N O P

11. If the two doors at the top are correct, which of those below are wrong?

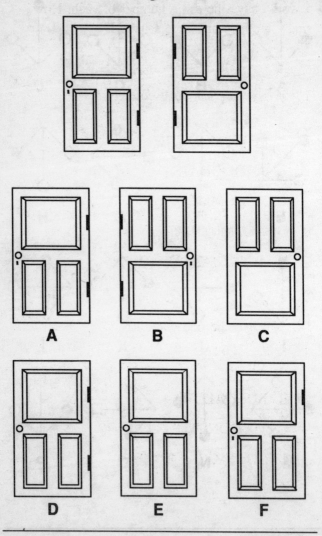

A   B   C

D   E   F

12. If I had one more sister I would have twice as many sisters as brothers. If I had one more brother I would have the same number of each. How many brothers and sisters have I?

13. Which word is spelt correctly?

    A. ACCOMODATE

    B. ACOMODATE

    C. ACCOMMODATE

    D. ACOMMODATE

    E. ACCOMADATE

14. Which is the odd one out?

    A. VILLA

    B. BUNGALOW

    C. MAISONETTE

    D. COTTAGE

15. Using your eyes only and without the aid of a pointer, trace which of the numbered lines will reach any of the goals marked A, B and C. State the number of the line and the goal reached. Right angles must be used only when there is no alternative route.

**NOW CHECK YOUR ANSWERS
AND KEEP A NOTE OF YOUR SCORE.**

Answers

1. C (Score 1 point)

The figures are transposed in the same way as in the example at the top.

2. C (Score 1 point)

The seat-retaining notches are cut the wrong way.

3. A. + +, B. x + or ÷ x or − +, C. x −, D. x x or + x (Score 1 point if all correct)

4. C (Score 1 point)

A, B and D all contain two circles, two squares, two straight lines and two triangles. In C there is only one triangle.

5. C (Score 1 point)

6. RICKS (Score 1 point)

The words are LIMERICKS and RICKSHAW.

7. 5 6 2 5 (Score 1 point)

The first number inside the brackets is the square root of the number outside the brackets. The remaining number inside the brackets is the square of the number outside the brackets.

8. They are all colours (Score 1 point if 8 or 9 correct; score 2 points if all correct)

A. BLACK, B. WHITE, C. BLUE, D. GREY, E. RED, F. SCARLET, G. GOLD, H. SILVER, I. GREEN, J. OLIVE.

9. F (Score 1 point)

This is an anagram of PLUM (a fruit); the others are anagrams of vegetables: A. POTATO, B. PEA, C. LEEK, D. TURNIP, E. SWEDE.

10. N (Score 1 point)

There are two black balls instead of one white and one black.

11. They are all wrong except A **(Score 1 point if all correct)**

B. Should not have a keyhole. C. Has no hinges. D. Should have a keyhole. E. Has neither a keyhole nor hinges. F. Has only one hinge

12. Three sisters and two brothers (Score 1 point if both correct)

This can be solved by simple deduction, but if algebra is used let x be the number of sisters and y the number of brothers:

$$x + 1 = 2y$$
$$y + 1 = x$$
Therefore, $y + 1 + 1 = 2y$
so $y = 2$
or $x + 1 = 2x - 2$
so $x = 3$

13. C (Score 1 point)

I believe this word is more often misspelt than it is spelt correctly, and I have seen all the variations at one time or another.

14. B. (Score 1 point)

The others each contain a double letter: A. VILLA, B. MAISONETTE, C. COTTAGE.

15. 3 – C **(Score 1 point if both correct)**

Line 1 finishes at 2, and line 2 finishes at 1.

REMEMBER TO KEEP A NOTE OF YOUR SCORE.

Notes: In Question 2 you would come an awful cropper if you sat on **that** deckchair! Question 12 was very easy, and ordinary deduction would have got you there even more quickly than algebra. Spelling, unfortunately, seems to be sadly neglected in modern education, and I have been astonished to find the word 'accommodation' is rarely spelt correctly.

Time limit: 20 minutes

1. A bag contains 64 balls of 8 different colours. There are 8 of each colour (including red). What is the least number you would have to pick, without looking, to be sure of selecting 3 red balls?

2. Arrange these shapes into four pairs.

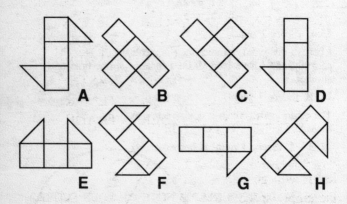

3. Can you think of two different words that will go into the brackets to link the first word with the second? For example, Cold (Storage) Heater.

FOOT (   ) FINDER

4. Select the number that is midway between the lowest number and the highest number. Which number is midway between that number and the number that is nearest to the highest number?

```
35   5 52 36 67
69   4 51 37 71
55 68  3 53 39
```

5. Starting with DELTA and choosing from the words listed, each word must begin with the last two letters of the previous word, finishing with DELTA.

D E L T A	ANGER	ORGAN
1. _ _ _ _ _	DINER	TABOR
2. _ _ _ _ _	ERODE	TAMER
3. _ _ _ _ _	ERRED	TASTE
4. _ _ _ _ _	ORATE	TENOR
5. D E L T A	ORDER	TRADE

6. Three different letters will go into the empty space to make three different words. You must give all three letters.

7. If this is ERTDAP

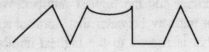

what is this?

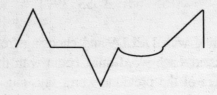

8. If this clock were turned 90 degrees anticlockwise, which of those below would appear? (Do not turn the page.)

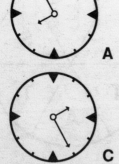

A

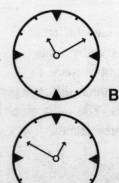

B

C

D

9. What word is this?

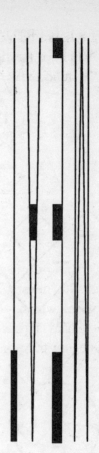

10. What goes into the empty brackets?

63 (5 9 4 2) 71
59 (7 1 6 3) 42
94 (4 2 5 9) 28
(_ _ _ _)

11. If the figure below were held in front of a mirror, which of the figures, A, B, C, D, E or F, would be reflected?

12. Which is the odd one out?

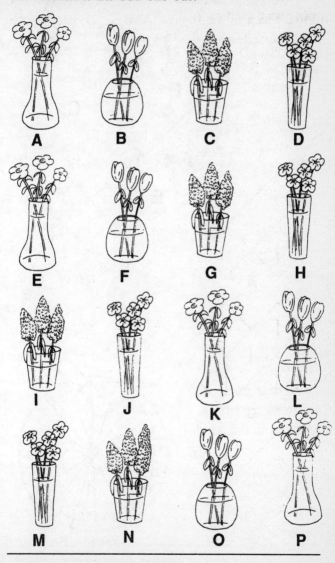

A B C D

E F G H

I J K L

M N O P

13. Literally speaking, can you make four pairs from these pictures?

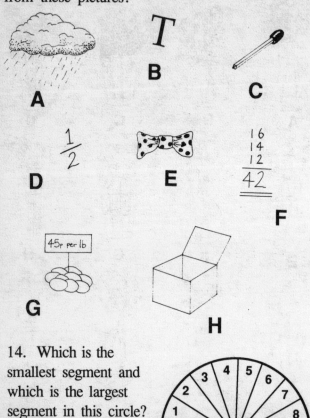

A

B

C

D $\frac{1}{2}$

E

```
 16
 14
 12
 42
```
F

45p per lb

G

H

14. Which is the smallest segment and which is the largest segment in this circle?

15. Which pipe is the odd one out?

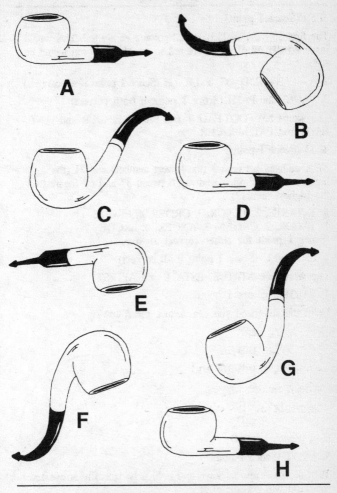

A

B

C

D

E

F

G

H

NOW CHECK YOUR ANSWERS
AND KEEP A NOTE OF YOUR SCORE.

Answers

1. 59 (Score 1 point)

The first 56 balls could be of all colours *except* red. This would leave 8 balls, all of which are red so any three chosen would be red.

2. A – F, B – C, D – G, and E – H (Score 1 point if all correct)

3. FAULT and PATH (Score 1 point if both correct)

The words are FOOT-FAULT and FAULT-FINDER and FOOT-PATH and PATH-FINDER.

4. 53 (Score 1 point)

37 is midway between 3 (the lowest number) and 71 (the highest number); 53 is midway between 37 and 69 (nearest to the highest number).

5. 1. TASTE, 2. TENOR, 3. ORDER, 4. ERODE **or**
1. TABOR, 2. ORGAN, 3. ANGER, 4. ERODE
(Score 1 point for either correct answer)

6. E, T and U (Score 1 point if all correct)

The words are STATUE, ESTATE and ATTEST.

7. PARTED (Score 1 point)

From the shorthand you can deduce the following

     ∧   is P
     –   is A
     ∨   is R
     ‿   is T
     ╱   is E
     | is D

8. A (Score 1 point)

9. MEAT (Score 1 point)

Turn the page upside down and hold it horizontally at eye level; the word will become clear.

10. 2 8 9 4 (Score 1 point)

The two numbers on the right of the *previous* brackets are the numbers on the left inside the brackets; the numbers on the left of the *previous* brackets are the numbers on the right inside the brackets.

11. F (Score 1 point)

Stripes go the opposite way when reflected in a mirror.

12. N (Score 1 point)

The fern is longer.

13. A – E RAIN BOW, B – F TEE TOTAL, C – H MATCH BOX, D – G HALF PRICE (Score 1 point if all correct)

14. 17 is the smallest segment; 14 is the largest segment (Score 1 point if both correct)

15. F (Score 1 point)

It has no silver band as on the other curved pipes.

REMEMBER TO KEEP A NOTE OF YOUR SCORE.

Notes: It was not easy in the limited time to think of all three of the letters that would satisfy Question 6, and the novel form of shorthand in Question 7 may have held you up for a while. I hope you didn't cheat by turning the page when you came to Question 8, although it would have been quite permissible to resort to subterfuge in Question 11. There was no restriction on holding the page to the light and viewing it from the other side!

1. A driving school claims an average test pass-rate of 76.8 per cent. What is the least number of pupils required to achieve this result?

2. Make a word from the missing letters of the alphabet.

3. What number completes the last number plate?

BIG 792	HCA 138

FED 456	EGH

4. Which row does not conform with the others?

A

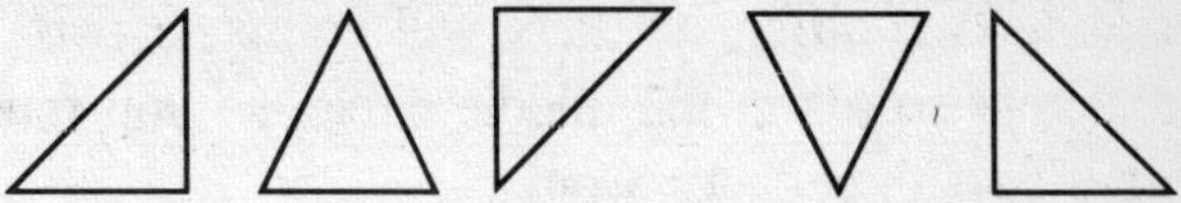

B

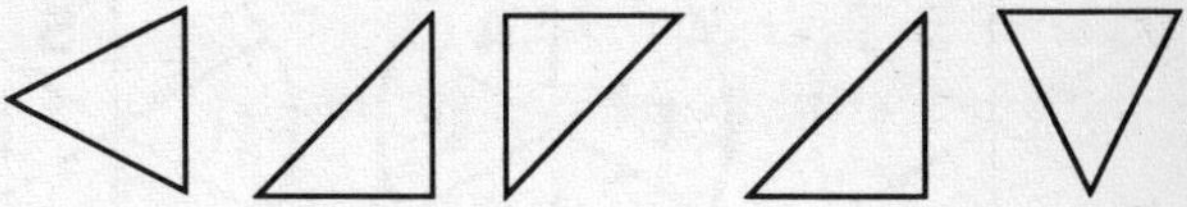

C

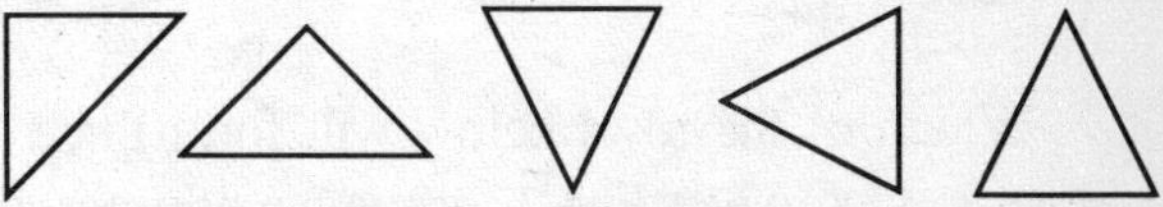

D

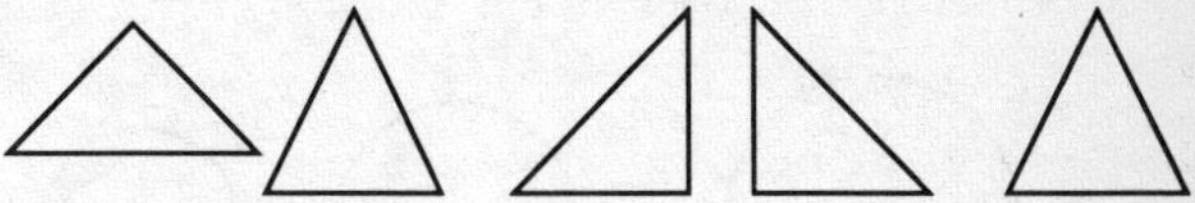

5. How many combinations of three or four of these numbers will add up to 50?

2   4   6   8   10   17   19   21   25

6. What comes next?

I   O   V   F   X   T   L   F   M   -

7. From the letters that will complete words in each of these circles, a three-letter word will result. Two different letters will complete two different words in the middle circle, so you must give two three-letter words.

8. Which of the rows below will form three perfect circles when line 1 – 2 is superimposed on line X – Y at the top?

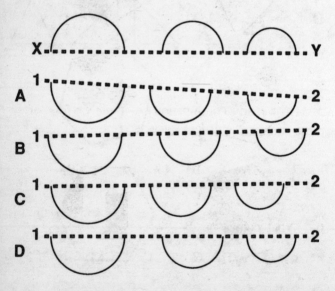

46

9. Six of these patterns can be arranged into three pairs. Which two will **not** make a matching pair?

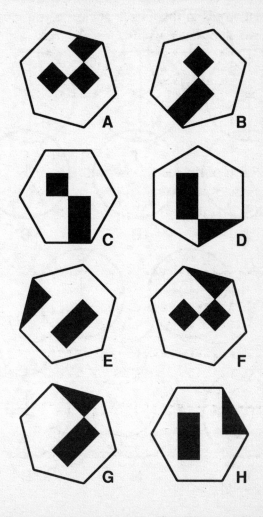

10. If the two clocks at the top are right, which of those below are wrong?

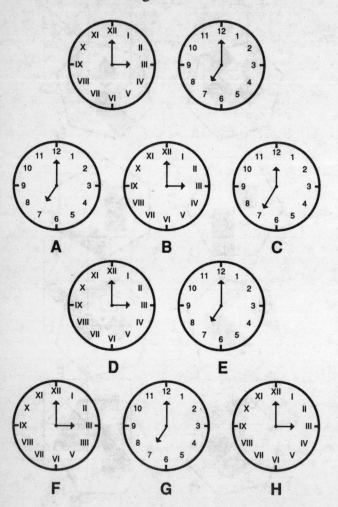

A

B

C

D

E

F

G

H

11.

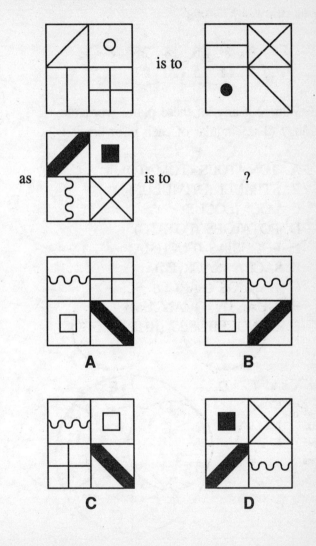

is to

as

is to

?

A

B

C

D

12. Which number in the bottom line comes next in the top line?

$$9 \quad 8 \quad 10 \quad 18 \quad 21 \quad 16 \quad -$$
$$14 \quad 15 \quad 20 \quad 27$$

13. Which, if any, of these plural words are wrong? (The singular of each is in brackets.)

  A. TOMATOES (TOMATO)
  B. STIMULI (STIMULUS)
  C. LOCI (LOCUS)
  D. POTATOES (POTATO)
  E. FUCHSIAS (FUCHSIA)
  F. SACRA (SACRUM)
  G. LARGOS (LARGO)
  H. QUANTA (QUANTUM)
  I. RHINOCEROSES (RHINOCEROS)

14. Give values for X and Y.

15. Which is the odd one out?

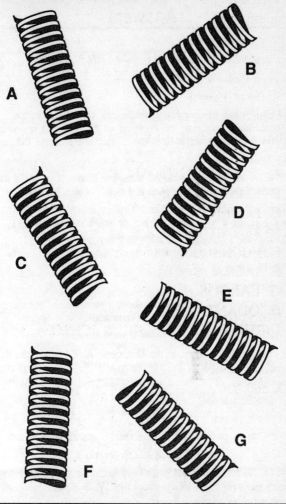

NOW CHECK YOUR ANSWERS
AND KEEP A NOTE OF YOUR SCORE.

51

Answers

1. 125 (Score 1 point)

96 passes out of 125 gives an average of 76.8 per cent.

2. MAZE (Score 1 point)

3. 875 (Score 1 point)

Give each letter the number according to its position in the alphabet. Then transpose the numbers so that the first becomes last and the last becomes first; the middle one remains the same.

4. C (Score 1 point)

In C there are two right-angled triangles. In the other rows there are three right-angled triangles and two isoceles triangles.

5. (Score 2 points if you found nine or more combinations; score 1 point if you found seven or eight combinations.)

Here are nine examples: 6 19 25; 8 17 25; 10 19 21; 4 21 25; 2 6 17 25; 2 4 19 25; 2 10 17 21; 4 10 17 19; 4 8 17 21.

6. T (Score 1 point)

The letters are the initials of the Roman numerals: I (One), V (Five), X (Ten), L (Fifty), M (Thousand).

7. ACT and ART (Score 1 point if both correct)

The missing letters are: in the first circle A (CASINO), in the second circle C or R (CINEMA or MARINE), in the third circle T (THESIS).

8. D (Score 1 point)

9. A and F (Score 1 point)

B and C are a pair; D and G are a pair; E and H are a pair.

10. C and F (Score 1 point if both correct)

In C the hour and minute hands have been transposed; in F the Roman numeral for 4 is IIII instead of IV.

11. A (Score 1 point)

The figures in the quarters are transposed as in the top example and their shading or patterns are transposed in the same way.

12. 27 **(Score 1 point)**

In the top line the first number, 9, is divisible by 3; 8 is divisible by 4; 10 is divisible by 5; 18 is divisible by 6; 21 is divisible by 7; 16 is divisible by 8. Hence the next number must be divisible by 9, and the only number that complies with this is 27.

13. They are ALL correct **(Score 1 point)**

14. X is 15 and Y is 11 **(Score 1 point if both correct)**

In the outer ring, going clockwise from 7, each number doubles the previous number and subtracts 1. Hence X (coming before 29) must be 15. In the inner ring, each number doubles the previous number and adds 1. Hence Y is 11 (double 5 plus 1).

15. C **(Score 1 point)**

The spiral turns the opposite way from the others.

REMEMBER TO KEEP A NOTE OF YOUR SCORE

Notes: There is little doubt that Question 5 held you up longer than the other questions.

NOW TOTAL YOUR SCORES FOR THE FIRST FOUR TESTS AND COMPARE THEM WITH THE RATINGS THAT FOLLOW.

Ratings in Group I

Test 1 – average 7 points
Test 2 – average 8 points
Test 3 – average 7 points
Test 4 – average 6 points

Out of a possible 62

Over 50	Excellent
40 – 50	Very Good
29 – 39	Good
28	Average
20 – 27	Fair
Under 20	Poor

Apart from a few questions, this was not a very difficult group of tests, especially for those who have tackled my earlier books. If you are a 'first-timer' at these tests you may have experienced some difficulty, possibly through a lack of understanding.

If your score was very low it would be a good idea to go through all the tests again in conjunction with the answers and explanations and try to fathom the reasoning that lies behind them. The tests that follow will become increasingly difficult and a very low score at this stage does not bode well. On the other hand, readers who have persevered with my earlier books should have found these tests very easy.

GROUP II
– More Difficult –

Test 1

Time limit: 1 hour
You may rest after 30 minutes and then
continue for a further 30 minutes.

1. This clock has gone mad! Every minute the
second hand goes back – first one second, then
two, then three and so on; the
minute hand goes forward
first two minutes, then
three, then four and
so on; the hour hand
goes back first three
hours, then four, then
five and so on. What
exact time will it
show five minutes
from now?

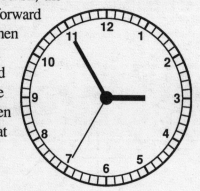

2. What is X?

17 24 93 14 X 31 41 39 42 71

3. Which letter should be in the brackets to end
the first word and start the second word?

MOUL (   ) HOW

56

4. Three trains start at different times on a 100-mile journey. Train A leaves 10 minutes late and stops at a station for 5 minutes. Its average speed when travelling is 40 mph. Train B leaves 20 minutes late and stops at a station for 14 minutes. Its average speed when travelling is 50 mph. Train C leaves 30 minutes late and stops at a station for 10 minutes. Its average speed when travelling is 50 mph. Which train completes the journey in the shortest time?

5. 6 3 7 4 is to G F D C as

is to

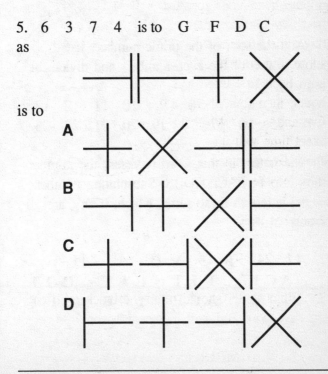

A

B

C

D

6. Which is the granny knot among the reef knots?

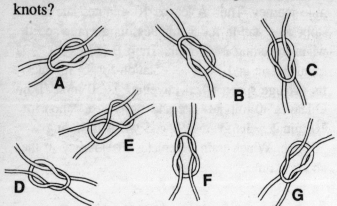

7. Add the sum of the prime numbers listed below to that of the even numbers and divide the result by 75.

4   5   6   7   8   9   10   11   12   13
14   15   16   17   18   19   20   21   22   23

8. The letters in this word represent the numbers from 1 to 9: FACETIOUS. Substituting numbers for the letters in these sums, which, if any, are wrong?

A.	B.	C.	D.
A C T	T I T	F I T	C O T
T I E	A C E	I C E	E F T
– – –	– – –	– – –	– – –

9. Working clockwise from SUN, supply words that will link the word preceding and the word following. (For example: RISING – SUN, which is already provided.)

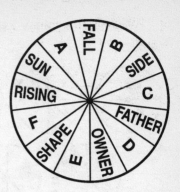

10. What is X?

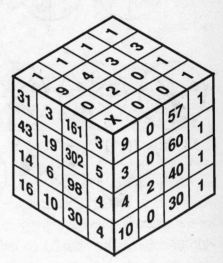

11. What is X?

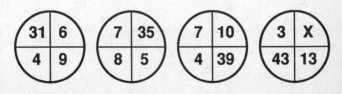

12. Which of the figures below comes after number 7?

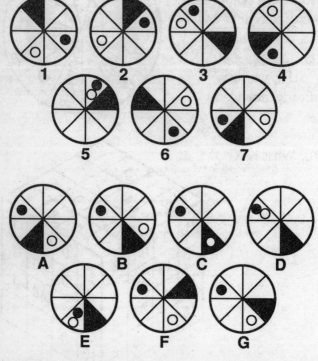

13. Find words that should go into the brackets to link the words that are outside the brackets.

A. Three (   ) men   F. Three (   ) road
B. Three (   ) mice   G. Three (   ) race
C. Three (   ) wood   H. Three (   ) limit
D. Three (   ) trick   I. Three (   ) suite
E. Three (   ) hat   J. Three (   ) landing

14. What are X, Y and Z?

15. Using two, three and four of these numbers, make three totals of 100:

5 9 17 19 22 36 41 42 64

Answers

1. 2 hours, 15 minutes, 20 seconds **(Score 1 point)**

2. 13 **(Score 1 point)**

Reverse each number from first to last or vice versa. X is the reverse of 31.

3. D **(Score 1 point)**

The words are MOULD and DHOW (an Arabian single-masted vessel, sometimes, but more rarely, spelt DOW).

4. B **(Score 1 point)**

A takes 2 hours, 45 minutes; B takes 2 hours, 34 minutes; C takes 2 hours, 40 minutes.

5. C **(Score 1 point)**

Substitute numbers for letters according to their alphabetic position. Thus, the first relationship is between 6 3 7 4 and 7 6 4 3. The figures at the bottom are transposed in the same order.

6. E **(Score 1 point)**

7. 3 **(Score 1 point)**

Prime numbers total 95; even numbers total 130; 225 divided by 75 is 3.

8. D is wrong **(Score 1 point)**

A.	B.	C.	D.
2 3 5	5 6 5	1 6 5	3 7 5
5 6 4	2 3 4	6 3 4	4 1 5
7 9 9	7 9 9	7 9 9	7 9 0

9. A. DOWN, B. OUT, C. STEP, D. LAND, E. SHIP, F. UP **(Score 1 point if all correct)**

10. 3 **(Score 1 point)**

Divide the totals of the left-hand facing columns by the totals of the corresponding right-hand facing columns to give the totals of the rows on the top face.

11. 6 (Score 1 point)

From the first circle the numbers move one segment clockwise into the next circle. The series are:

31	35	39	43	(adding 4 each time)
6	5	4	3	(subtracting 1 each time)
9	8	7	6(X)	(subtracting 1 each time)
4	7	10	13	(adding 3 each time)

12. C (Score 1 point)

The black segment moves clockwise, first to the next segment, then missing one, then two and so forth. The black spot moves in the same way, but anti-clockwise. The white spot moves clockwise, one segment at a time.

13. A. wise, B. blind, C. ply, D. card, E. cornered, F. lane, G. legged, H. mile, I. piece, J. point **(Score 2 points if all correct; score 1 point if 8 or 9 correct)**

14. X is 10, Y is 6, Z is 4 (Score 1 point if all correct)
In the first circle add numbers in opposite segments: 20, 19, 18, 17 (X being 10). In the second circle 16, 15, 14, 13 (Y being 6). In the third circle 12, 11, 10, 9 (Z being 4).

15. 64 and 36; 64, 19 and 17 *or* 41, 42 and 17 *or* 42, 36 and 22; 5, 9, 22 and 64 **(Score 1 point if you solved totals with two, three and four numbers)**

REMEMBER TO KEEP A NOTE OF YOUR SCORE.

Notes: At first glance, Question 2 seemed to contain nothing to lead to the answer, although it probably became clear when you realized that the numbers were reversed from front to back. In Question 13 you may have failed with E (three-cornered hat) or H (three-mile limit). It was not too difficult to find at least one example of combinations of two, three and four numbers to total 100 in Question 15.

Test 2

Time limit: 45 minutes

1. What is X?

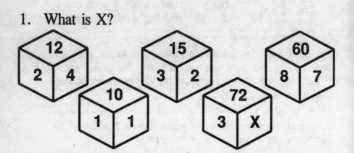

2. Give values for X and Y.

O	X	□	□	21
O	□	O	O	15
X	X	X	O	5
X	O	X	□	Y
6	**13**	**13**	**X**	

3. What can you make of this?

HEW
HO
HE
SIT
AT
E
SIS
LO
ST

4. Where are these?

    A. RAIN
    B. PAINS
    C. REGALIA

5. Which of these statements are true and which false?

A. When a car is driven forwards the wheels rotate anti-clockwise.

B. If a clock is put forward $1\frac{1}{4}$ hours the minute hand moves through 450 degrees.

C. When a clock reads 4.10 the acute angle between the hands is exactly 60 degrees.

6. Pair each word in the first column with a word in the second column.

A.	TEST	1.	CLASS
B.	SAFETY	2.	RAISING
C.	HAIR	3.	TEAM
D.	SELF	4.	BOY
E.	HOME	5.	MATCH
F.	CRICKET	6.	MATE
G.	HIGH	7.	NET
H.	FIRST	8.	FIRST
I.	PLAY	9.	BALL
J.	TALL	10.	HELP

7. What four-letter word comes next?

CHAIN
INCH
CHINAMAN
ANCHOR
ORANGE
GEORGIAN
ANGEL
????

8. Which is the odd one out?

   A. 119   B. 153   C. 136   D. 147   E. 102

9. If

is Gerald and...

is William,

who is this?

10. Which is the odd one out?

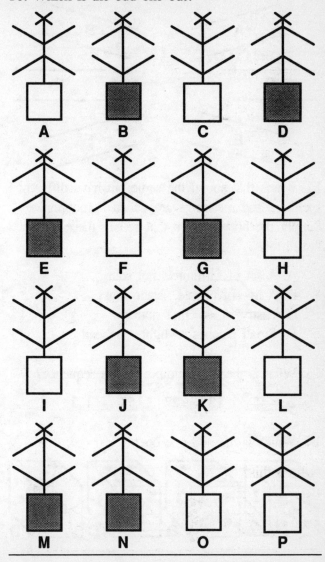

11. Which is the odd one out?

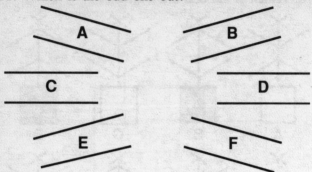

12. Words that sound the same but have different spellings and meanings are called homophones. Supply the homophones that satisfy these definitions.

    A. A set of furniture...not sour
    B. A line of people...stage hint
    C. Pastry mass...first note
    D. Small patches of light...to bend

13. What is the next number in this sequence?

    2   5   12   27   58   121   ?

14. Which is the odd one out?

15. A. Which route gives the highest total?
    B. Which route gives the lowest total?

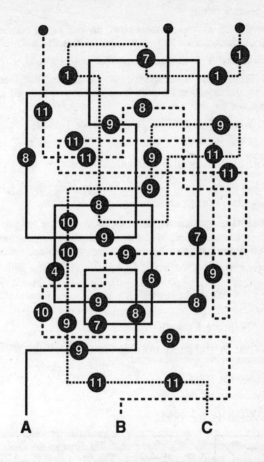

Answers

1. 9 (Score 1 point)

Divide the top number by the sum of the two facing numbers and the series becomes 2, 3, 4, 5 and 6 (if X is 9).

2. X is 22 and Y is 13 (Score 1 point if both correct)

Fairly simple deduction, especially if you realized that there were no alternatives in the third horizontal row, which led to the solution for the first vertical row.

3. HE WHO HESITATES IS LOST (Score 1 point)

4. A. IRAN, B. SPAIN, C. ALGERIA   (Score 1 point if all correct)

The words are anagrams of the countries.

5. A. FALSE, B. TRUE, C. FALSE   (Score 1 point if all correct)

The near-side wheels rotate anti-clockwise, but the off-side wheels rotate clockwise! In C the acute angle is slightly more than 60 degrees, because by the time the minute hand reaches 10, the hour hand will have moved slightly past the figure 4.

6. A – 5, B – 8, C – 7, D – 2, E – 10, F – 3, G – 9, H – 1, I – 6 and J – 4 (Score 2 points if all correct; score 1 point if 8 correct)

7. ELAN (Score 1 point)

Each word starts with the last two letters followed by the first two letters of the previous word.

8. D (Score 1 point)

All the others are divisible by 17.

9. DAVID (Score 1 point)

The totals of the dots on the dice represent consonants according to their position in the alphabet **omitting vowels**; the totals of the spots on the dominoes represent vowels: A – 1, E – 2, I – 3, O – 4 and U – 5.

10. J (Score 1 point)

The upper branches should point downwards, as in D, E and N.

11. E (Score 1 point)

The lines are not parallel, as they are in all the others.

12. A. SUITE and SWEET, B. QUEUE and CUE, C. DOUGH and DOH, D. FLECKS and FLEX (Score 1 point if all correct)

13. 248 (Score 1 point)

Each number is double the previous number plus 1, then 2, 3, 4, 5 and finally 6; double 121 and add 6.

14. B (Score 1 point)

The only dice that has no centre spot. Alternatively, the spots add to 10 whereas all the others add to 9.

15. A. C, B. A. A scores 99, B scores 100, C scores 107. (Score 1 point if both correct)

REMEMBER TO KEEP A NOTE OF YOUR SCORE.

Notes: Question 2 was very easy, requiring only basic deduction. You may even have considered it too easy for this group, but 'one man's meat...'. Surprisingly, even when a phrase is all too familiar it can take on a new aspect when it is spaced differently, as in Question 3.

The anagrams in Question 4 were easy except for C, but you may have been caught out in Question 5 by A and C. If you plunged straight in without giving a second thought to these problems, you may have assumed that all the wheels of a car rotate in the same direction and that at 4.10 the hour hand is exactly on the figure 4.

Test 3

Time limit: 1 hour
You may rest after 30 minutes and
then continue for another 30 minutes.

1. There are 134 sweets coloured red and white in a bag. If there were two fewer red ones there would be twice as many red ones as white ones. How many of each colour are there?

2. If ACCORD is 200500, and VIVISECTION is 661001, what is ALLUVIAL?

3. What is X?

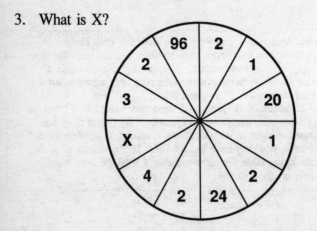

4. Which is the odd one out?
   A. COMMON
   B. PHARISEES
   C. HAGGARD
   D. FOLLOWER
   E. GOOGLY
   F. NOON
   G. APPAL
   H. FELLOW

5. Insert one extra letter into the words defined on the left to make words that fit the definition on the right:
   A. Off course...receptacle for smokers
   B. More courageous...large rock
   C. About...stranded
   D. Child's plaything...quaintly humorous
   E. Uncivilized...rescue

6. Pair these syllables to make 10 words.
   A. CAR   1. SON
   B. SIL   2. NET
   C. TER   3. CID
   D. HOR   4. TON
   E. HER   5. DOM
   F. TEN   6. ROR
   G. PAR   7. VER
   H. DAM   8. MIT
   I. SEL   9. DON
   J. RAN   10. AGE

7.

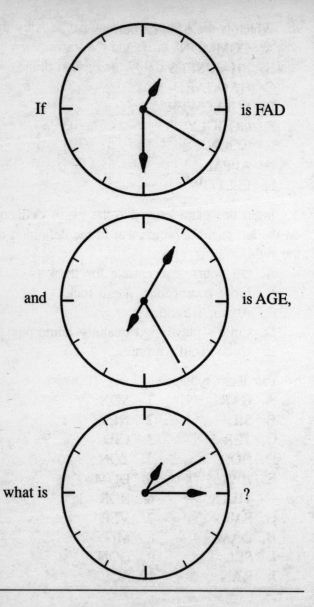

If ⟨clock⟩ is FAD

and ⟨clock⟩ is AGE,

what is ⟨clock⟩ ?

8. Multiply the lowest even number in A by the highest odd number in B; add the lowest even number in C and divide by the highest prime number in D.

7	8	9
10	6	11
1	5	3

A

74	66	70
65	67	72
66	69	68

B

7	5	6
9	8	4
3	1	10

C

3	8	11	14
15	7	9	21
13	19	16	18

D

9. Which is the odd one out?
   A. MELODEON
   B. BELGIAN
   C. PEDLAR
   D. APPLICABLE
   E. PLUTONIUM

10. What goes into the empty brackets?
        1 4 7 (7 2) 3 1 2
          5 5 (1 1 0) 2 1 8
        1 1 1 (   ) 2

11. Which is the odd one out?
    A. MATCHBOX
    B. FRENCHMAN
    C. ETCHED
    D. DUTCHMAN
    E. PATCHING
    F. URCHIN

12. Decide which of these statements are true and which are false.
    A. Sydney is the capital of Australia.
    B. Julius Caesar invaded Britain in 55 BC.
    C. Beethoven wrote only one opera.
    D. Gauguin was a Spanish post-impressionist painter.

13. Arrange these into 4 pairs:

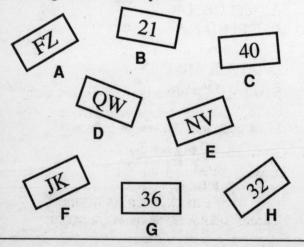

FZ
A

21
B

40
C

QW
D

NV
E

JK
F

36
G

32
H

14. Supply words that will link the words on each side – e.g., part (TIME) piece.

A. RED
——
SIDE

B. ——
MAN

C. ——
STAMP

D. ——
FREE

E. ——
MAIDEN

F. ——
LAND

G. ——
BIRD

H. ——
TOWEL

I. ——
WAY

J. ——
ROBE

15. One of these is **not** a play by Shakespeare:
   A. *The Two Gentlemen from Verona*
   B. *Coriolanus*
   C. *Measure for Measure*
   D. *King John*

NOW CHECK YOUR ANSWERS
AND KEEP A NOTE OF YOUR SCORE.

Answers

1. 90 red sweets, 44 white sweets **(Score 1 point if both correct)**

You probably solved this by elementary deduction, which, unusually, might have proved quicker than by algebra. Deduct 2 from 134, divide by 3 (to give white sweets) multiply by 2 and add 2 to give the red sweets. If you use algebra: let x be the number of red sweets and y the number of white sweets.

$$
\begin{aligned}
x + y &= 134 \\
x - 2 &= 2y
\end{aligned}
$$

$$
\begin{aligned}
\text{therefore} \quad 2y &= 134 - y - 2 \\
\text{so} \quad 3y &= 132 \\
\text{and} \quad y &= 44 \\
\text{then} \quad x + 44 &= 134 \\
\text{and} \quad x &= 90
\end{aligned}
$$

2. 5050650 **(Score 1 point)**

Substitute modern numbers for Roman numerals: aCCorD (200, 500); VIVIseCtIon (6,6,100,1); and, aLLuVIaL (50, 50, 6, 50).

3. 5 **(Score 1 point)**

Starting at 3 and moving clockwise, numbers in the upper half paired with opposite numbers in the lower half equal 4, by first adding, then multiplying and then dividing. This sequence is repeated, so that 20 (opposite to X) must be divided by 5 (the value of X) to give 4.

4. H. **(Score 1 point)**

All the others contain a double letter sandwiched between two identical letters:

A. cOMMOn	B. phariSEES	C. hAGGArd
D. fOLLOwer	E. GOOGly	F. NOON
G. APPAl	H. fELLOw	

In H there is also a double letter (L) but it is sandwiched between two different letters (E and O).

5. A. ASTRAY...ASHTRAY, B. BOLDER...BOULDER, C. AROUND...AGROUND, D. DOLL...DROLL, E. SAVAGE...SALVAGE **(Score 1 point if all correct)**

6. A – 4 (CARTON), B – 7 (SILVER), C – 6 (TERROR), D – 2 (HORNET), E – 8 (HERMIT), F – 9 (TENDON), G – 1 (PARSON), H – 10 (DAMAGE), I – 5 (SELDOM), J – 3 (RANCID) **(Score 2 points if all correct; score 1 point if 8 correct)**

7. CAB **(Score 1 point)**

The minute hand denotes the first letter by substituting a letter for the number according to its alphabetical order – 3 is C. The hour hand denotes the second letter – 1 is A. The second hand denotes the third letter – 2 is B.

8. 22 **(Score 1 point)**

6 multiplied by 69 is 414; 414 added to 4 is 418; 418 divided by 19 is 22.

9. B **(Score 1 point)**

In the others the first letters combined with the last letters give fruits: A. MELodeON (MELON), C. PEdlAR (PEAR), D. APPlicabLE (APPLE), E. PLutoniUM (PLUM). In B they give a vegetable: BElgiAN (BEAN).

10. 6 **(Score 1 point)**

Multiply the sums of the digits on each side of the brackets: 12 (the sum of 1, 4 and 7) multiplied by 6 (the sum of 3, 1 and 2) equals 72 (inside the first brackets); 10 (the sum of 5 and 5) multiplied by 11 (the sum of 2, 1 and 8) equals 110 (inside the second brackets); 3 (the sum of 1, 1 and 1) multiplied by 2 (on the right side of the brackets) equals 6 (inside the third brackets).

11. B **(Score 1 point)**

In all the others CH occurs exactly in the middle.

12. A. FALSE, B. TRUE, C. TRUE, D. FALSE **(Score 1 point if all correct)**

Canberra is the capital of Australia; Gauguin was a *French* post-impressionist painter.

13. A – H, B – F, C – D, E – G **(Score 1 point if all correct)**

Give the letters numbers according to their position in the alphabet and pair them with their corresponding numbers: FZ equals 32, JK equals 21, QW equals 40 and NV equals 36.

14. A. SEA, B. SHOW, C. DATE, D. DUTY, E. HAND, F. OVER, G. LADY, H. BATH, I. RAIL, J. WARD (Score 2 points if all correct; score 1 point if 8 or 9 correct)

15. A (Score 1 point)

The correct title is: *The Two Gentlemen* of *Verona*.

REMEMBER TO KEEP A NOTE OF YOUR SCORE.

Notes: Questions 6, 8, 13 and 14 were the most time-consuming, for which allowance was made in the time limit that was imposed. In Question 15 you probably thought *King John* was not one of Shakespeare's plays. It is indeed, although it is rarely performed. The subtle difference in the title of *The Two Gentlemen of Verona* may have caught you out.

Test 4

Time limit: 65 minutes
You may rest after 35 minutes and
then continue for a further 30 minutes.

1. Which is the odd one out and why?

2. What is X?

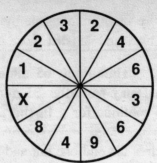

3. Name the cities or towns that go into the brackets to complete words. The number of letters in each name is indicated by dashes.

A. C O M (_ _ _ _ _ _) O N
B. S U B (_ _ _ _ _) T E
C. I R (_ _ _ _ _) T E
D. D I (_ _ _ _ _) M
E. M A (_ _ _ _ _ _) G

4. What is X?

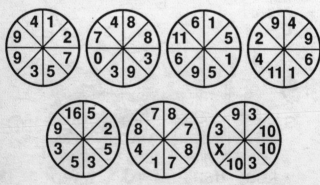

5. Add the numbers divisible by 7 to those divisible by 9 and subtract those divisible by 11.

6. What is X?

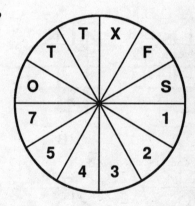

7. Arrange these words into eight pairs.

AGE	AIR	DAY	HOUSE
LIGHT	LOT	MATE	MESS
ON	PASS	PORT	RAY
ROBE	SHIP	TO	WARD

8. If the top house is correct, which, if any, of those below have been constructed wrongly?

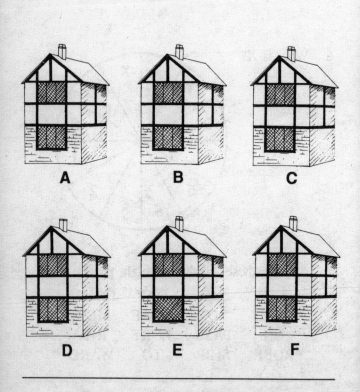

A   B   C

D   E   F

9. Alf, Bert and Charlie played a round of golf. Their combined score was 257. Alf took two more strokes than Charlie; Bert took seven more strokes than Alf; Charlie took two strokes fewer than Alf. What did each man score?

10. Match these words into 10 pairs:

A. JET	1. MASTER
B. GAS	2. TOWER
C. MAN	3. GLORY
D. WHITE	4. HEAD
E. BLUE	5. LAG
F. BELL	6. VOTE
G. BLOCK	7. BAG
H. SHIP'S	8. HOUSE
I. MAJORITY	9. COLLAR
J. OLD	10. SLAUGHTER

11. The black ball moves one place at a time clockwise; the white ball moves one place at a time anti-clockwise; the cross moves two places at a time anti-clockwise. In how many moves will they all be together?

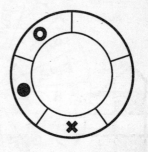

12. Copy this grid (time allowed for) and supply words to satisfy the definitions. The vertical word in the centre means a native of a Greek island.

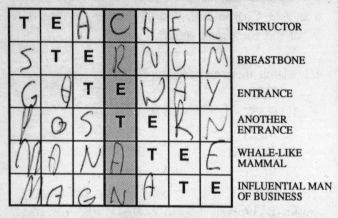

T	E	A	C	H	E	R	INSTRUCTOR
S	T	E	R	N	U	M	BREASTBONE
G	A	T	E	W	A	Y	ENTRANCE
P	O	S	T	E	R	N	ANOTHER ENTRANCE
M	A	N	A	T	E	E	WHALE-LIKE MAMMAL
M	A	G	N	A	T	E	INFLUENTIAL MAN OF BUSINESS

13. Give words which will link other words in a clockwise direction, as, for example, BIRD and BATH, which are already inserted.

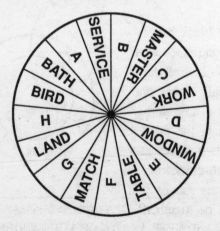

SERVICE B MASTER C WORK D WINDOW E TABLE F MATCH G LAND H BIRD BATH A

14. What is X?

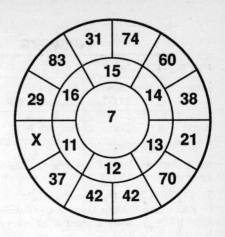

15. Five different letters will go into the empty space to complete five different words. You must give all five words.

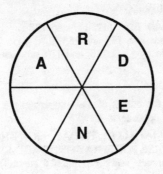

Answers

1. G **(Score 1 point)**

All the others begin with C and end with R: A. CASTOR, B. CIGAR, C. CLOVER, D. CALENDAR, E. COLLAR, F. CORNER, H. CHAIR, I. CAR. G is a COMMA, which begins with C but does not end with R.

2. 12 **(Score 1 point)**

Move clockwise from 1 and miss two segments each time. The series are: $1 - 2 - 3 - 4, 2 - 4 - 6 - 8, 3 - 6 - 9 - 12(X)$.

3. A. PARIS (com-PARIS-on), B. LIMA (sub-LIMA-te), C. RIGA (ir-RIGA-te), D. AGRA (di-AGRA-m), E. TURIN (ma-TURIN-g) **(Score 1 point if all correct)**

4. 4 **(Score 1 point)**

Add alternate segments throughout: first circle = 20, second circle = 21, third circle = 22, fourth circle = 23, fifth circle = 24, sixth circle = 25. Therefore, alternate segments in the seventh circle should add to 26.

5. 687 **(Score 1 point)**

Those divisible by 7 are 112, 147 and 133 (total 392). Those divisible by 9 are 117, 135 and 153 (total 405). The only number divisible by 11 is 110, and 110 subtracted from 797 gives 687.

6. F **(Score 1 point)**

The letters are the initials of the numbers in the opposite segments. X is opposite to 4.

7. AIR-SHIP, MATE-LOT, TO-DAY, LIGHT-HOUSE, MESS-AGE, PASS-PORT, RAY-ON, WARD-ROBE **(Score 2 points if all correct: score 1 point if 6 correct)**

8. D and E **(Score 1 point if both correct)**

In D the chimney is different; in E the bottom window is not divided.

9. Alf took 84 strokes, Bert took 91 strokes and Charlie took 82 strokes **(Score 1 point if all correct)**

10. A – 5, B – 7, C – 10, D – 8, E – 9, F – 2, G – 4, H – 1, I – 6, J – 3 **(Score 2 points if all correct; score 1 point if 8 correct)**

11. 3 moves **(Score 1 point)**

12. TEACHER, STERNUM, GATEWAY, POSTERN, MANATEE, MAGNATE **(Score 1 point if all correct)**

The vertical word in the centre is CRETAN.

13. A. ROOM, B. STATION, C. PIECE, D. SHOP, E. DRESSING, F. TENNIS, G. WOOD, H. LADY **(Score 1 point if all correct)**

14. 40 **(Score 1 point)**

In each segment add the two numbers in the outer circle and divide by the number in the inner circle. In each case the answer is 7, as in the centre.

15. RAINED, GARDEN, ARDENT, WARDEN and HARDEN **(Score 1 point if all correct)**

REMEMBER TO KEEP A NOTE OF YOUR SCORE

Notes: Questions 3, 4 and 5 probably delayed you, while in Question 6 the fact that the letters were the initials of the numbers either came to you quickly or had you baffled. In spite of the elaborate architecture in Question 8, the differences probably gave you little difficulty. In Question 15 GARDEN, WARDEN, HARDEN and ARDENT were fairly obvious, but RAINED may have held you up.

NOW TOTAL YOUR SCORES FOR THE FOUR TESTS IN THIS GROUP AND COMPARE THEM WITH THE RATINGS THAT FOLLOW.

Ratings in Group II

Test 1 – average 7 points
Test 2 – average 9 points
Test 3 – average 7 points
Test 4 – average 8 points

Out of a possible 66
Over 49   Excellent
39 – 48   Very good
32 – 38   Good
      31   Average
27 – 30   Fair
Under 30   Poor

Some of these problems were pretty tough, and the scores were kept low by the strict time limits. I have always been amazed to find in pre-testing, that a problem that will completely baffle one person – however long is spent on it – will be solved almost immediately by another. Those gifted in numeracy are often caught out by a problem in another subject, which may be quickly solved by someone with no particular ability in numeracy. Because the number of problems devoted to each subject is almost equal, the overall ratings give a reliable indication of 'intelligence' in its broadest sense and insofar as that word can be defined.

GROUP III
– Difficult –

Time limit: 1¹/₂ hours
You may rest after 45 minutes
and then resume for another 45 minutes.

1. This problem can be solved by using skilful verbal deduction. Copy the grid and then complete the crossword puzzle in which numbers have been substituted for letters. One letter is provided, and the only clue is that one of the words is UMBRAGE.

1	2	3	4	5	1	4
5		10		1		8
9	3	4		10	11	12
9		1	3	4		13
14	15	5		5	16	8
15		16		17 N		8
18	1	15	5	18	15	18

2. What is X?

F W R R I I A L C N
L H C I A I A R S M
      X

3. Which is the odd one out, and why?

    A. For climatic reasons, kangaroos, zebras, cheetahs and jackasses are not quite what you would expect to be native to this country.

    B. The quick brown fox jumped over the lazy dog.

    C. Monkeys, leopards, giraffes, jaguars, are to be found in zoos everywhere – that's quite expected.

4. What is X?

    21 8 46 X 2 92 16 42

5. What goes into the brackets?

1	5	8	(	9	3	12	)	2	7	1
3	1	6	(	9	8	4	)	7	3	1
1	2	3	(				)	4	5	6

6. What is X?

13 4 −̲ 5 1	4 − 5̲ 1 8	− 5 1̲ 8 9
A	**B**	**C**

0 3 −̲ 6 12	8 0 3̲ − 6	7 8 0̲ 3 −
A	**B**	**C**

5 1 8̲ 9 13	1 8 9̲ 13 4	8 9 13̲ 4 −
D	**E**	**F**

12 7 8̲ 0 3	6 12 7̲ 8 0	− 6 X̲ 7 8
D	**E**	**F**

7. What is X?

3	7	5	2	1
1	2	8	9	3
4	1	6	7	12
5	5	**X**	5	5
7	7	7	1	1
4	4	4	4	2

8. What are X and Y?

X   19   13   8   4   1   3   6   10   15   Y

9. If ◯ is RUBBER, what are the other two words?

F (E)(B)(R)(U) A (R) Y

Sun	Mon	Tue	Wed	Thu	Fri	Sat
		__1__	2	3	4	5
6	7	8	9	10	11	12
13	14	15	__16__	17	18	19
20	21	22	23	24	__25__	26
27	28					

10. Arrange these pictures into eight pairs.

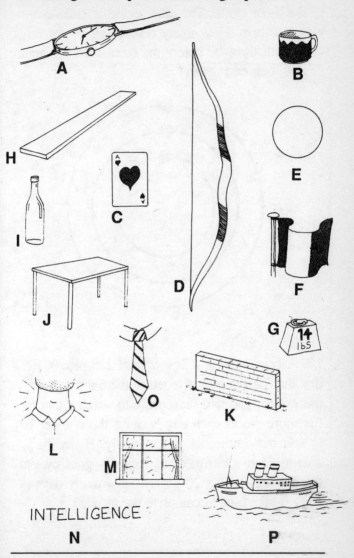

A

B

H

C

D

E

I

F

J

G

L

O

K

M

N INTELLIGENCE

P

11. The diameter of the outer circle is twice that of the inner circle. The other circle is midway between them. How many revolutions of the inner circle will there be before the three balls are again in line with each other?

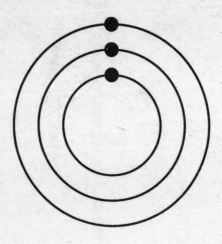

12. A boy is doing a jigsaw with 275 pieces. Each day that he fits pieces together there are fewer pieces left, and it is reasonable to assume that he fits more pieces each day because the number left to sort out diminishes progressively. Hence he is able to fit an *extra* piece as each day goes by. On the first day he fits 20 pieces. How many days does it take him to complete the puzzle?

13. How far is SOUTHBURY?

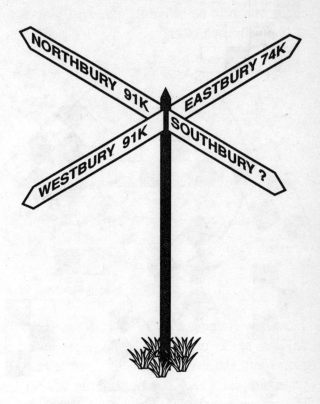

14. Which two pieces will complete the chequered square?

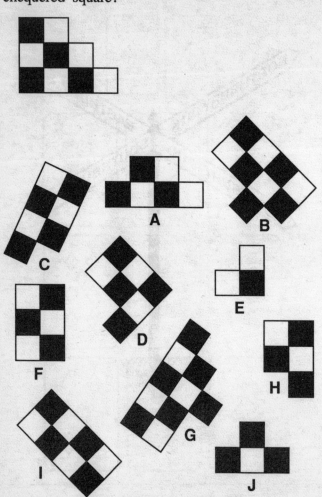

15. The two cards at the top should enable you to deduce the word represented by the cards below.

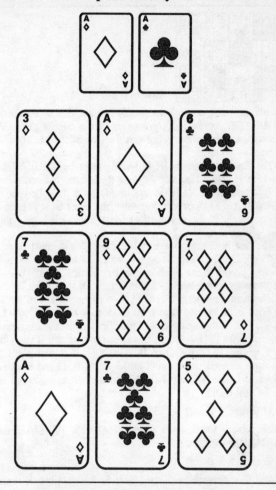

NOW CHECK YOUR ANSWERS
AND KEEP A NOTE OF YOUR SCORE.

Answers

1.

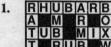

(Score 1 point)

As all the other seven-letter words contain double numbers, UMBRAGE can be quickly inserted in the correct place. The letters contained in that word can then be allotted to their respective squares.

The first word across [R–UBARB] must be RHUBARB, so 2 must be H. Now consider the first three-letter horizontal word –UB. It cannot be RUB (already used), so it must be cub, dub, hub, nub, pub, sub or tub. Whatever the letter is, it is used twice consecutively in the first vertical word, and so it is probably T, thus giving RATTLED.

The last horizontal line contains three Ds, so must be DREADED. The third vertical word is ARMBAND (N is already given). Now consider the last vertical word [B———D]. As there are two identical letters before D, they must be vowels.

The final three-letter word [M – –] cannot end with A, B, D, G, N, R or T, as they have been used, so it must end with C, P, W, X or Y. Substituting these letters in turn in the remaining vertical word [BO– –OOD] makes it obvious that it must be X or Y, giving BOYHOOD or BOXWOOD. If it were the latter the three lettered word would be M–X. A, E, O and U can be eliminated, leaving only I (MIX), so the remaining word must be BOXWOOD.

2. D (Score 1 point)

Taking every fourth letter gives: FRANCIS, WILLIAM and RICHARD.

3. B (Score 1 point)

A and C each contain all the letters of the alphabet. B does **not** contain all the letters because S is missing!

4. 1 (**Score 1 point**)

The first number is half the last one. The second number is half the penultimate one, and so on. Therefore $X(1)$ is half of 2.

5. 4 10 7 (**Score 1 point**)

Add the first and last digits of the number on the left and place the result on the left inside the brackets. Add the first and last digits of the number on the right and place the answer next inside the brackets. Then add the middle numbers of those outside the brackets and place the answer on the right inside the brackets. Thus, in the last line: add 1 to 3 (4),4 to 6 (10) and 2 to 5 (7).

6. 12 (**Score 1 point**)

Although the numbers on the globes indicate the direction of rotation, they are immaterial and are in the nature of being 'red herrings'. The important numbers are the middle ones (enclosed in squares).

The second line has the same letters as the first, and this indicates that the two lines must be regarded as a pair and the two centre numbers added together. This gives (after the first globes, which add to zero): 8, 1, 16, 16, 13 plus the value of X. Substituting letters of the alphabet according to the numbers gives: H, A, P, P, Y. As Y is the 25th letter of the alphabet and 13 is in the centre of the top globe, the bottom globe must show 12 to bring the total to 25.

7. 10 (**Score 1 point**)

The top row gives the same total (18) as the bottom row. The second row from the top gives the same total (23) as the second row from the bottom. Therefore the third row from the top must give the same total as the third row from the bottom, so X must be 10 to bring the total to 30.

8. X is 26, Y is 21 (**Score 1 point if both correct**)

Starting at the middle, at 1, the right-hand side progresses: 1, 3, 6, 10, 15, (21) the value of Y (the difference increasing by 1 each time).

The left-hand side progresses: 1, 4, 8, 13, 19, (26) the value of X (the difference increasing by 1 each time)

9. BOTTLE and APPLY (Score 1 point if both correct)

The symbols indicate letters by substituting letters according to their alphabetical order for the numbers enclosed or underlined by the symbols. A double symbol indicates a double letter. Thus in RUBBER, a circle encloses the letters E, B, U and R. There are two circles around B because it indicates BB, and the anagram of E, BB, U and R, R (ringed twice) is RUBBER.

Following the symbol ☐

    2   5   12   15   20 (double):

    B   E   L   O   TT (BOTTLE)

Following the underlining

    1   12   16 (underlined twice)   25

    A   L   PP   Y (APPLY)

10. A – N (WATCH WORD), B – 0 (CUP TIE), C – H (CARD BOARD), D – M (BOW WINDOW), E – J (ROUND TABLE), F – P (FLAG SHIP), G – K (STONE WALL), I – L (BOTTLE NECK) **(Score 1 point if all correct)**

11. Six revolutions (Score 1 point)

If x is the circumference of the inner circle, the others are $^{3x}/_2$ and $^2/_x$ respectively.

12. 11 days (Score 1 point)

	Pieces fitted	Pieces left to fit		Pieces fitted	Pieces left to fit
1st day	20	255	7th day	26	114
2nd day	21	234	8th day	27	87
3rd day	22	212	9th day	28	59
4th day	23	189	10th day	29	30
5th day	24	165	11th day	30	–
6th day	25	140			

13. 86 kilometres (Score 1 point)

Give consonants a number according to their position in the alphabet, **omitting vowels**. Give vowels these values: A – 1, E – 2, I – 3, O – 4 and U – 5.

14. A and G (Score 1 point if both correct)

15. CASTIGATE (Score 1 point)

The top two cards represent letters: diamonds 1 to King (1-13) – that is, A to M; clubs 1 to king (14 - 26) – that is, N to Z. The bottom cards therefore represent: 3 diamonds – C, Ace of diamonds – A, 6 clubs – S, 7 clubs – T, 9 diamonds – I, 7 diamonds – G, Ace of diamonds – A, 7 clubs – T, 5 diamonds – E.

REMEMBER TO KEEP A NOTE OF YOUR SCORE.

Notes: A very tough test, this. As you will see when you compare your final ratings, average scores were extremely low – and small wonder! So don't be despondent if you have registered a low score.

Question 1 may have caused a certain amount of brain fatigue and have taken considerable time, especially with having to copy the grid, although ample time was allowed for this. I hope you followed the reasoning explained in the answer.

In Question 3 you almost certainly jumped to the conclusion that B was **not** the odd one out. Most people know that a sentence often used to test a typewriter is: 'The quick brown fox jumps over the lazy dog'. But using the word 'jumped' instead of 'jumps' eliminated the 's'. Because of this presumption, you probably did not bother to check the other sentences, when you would have found that they did, indeed, contain all the letters of the alphabet.

Question 12 probably took you a long time to work out, and probably entailed much writing. The fiendish idea I had of omitting the vowels from the alphabetical order of the consonants may have given rise to a further brainstorm in Question 13.

Question 15 may not have been too difficult for those of you who have read my previous books. I hit on the idea that there are 26 cards in two suits of playing cards as well as 26 letters in the alphabet some time ago and have not hesitated to use this ploy since.

Time limit: 1 hour
You may rest after 30 minutes and then
resume for a further 30 minutes.

1. When the black
pinion has made $3\frac{1}{2}$
revolutions clockwise,
where will the tooth
marked X be on the the
white pinion?

2. Which letter in the bottom row belongs with those in the top row?

NC

OYZLM

3. What is the total of the numbers that are squares of whole numbers?

24	38	117	16	128	46
245	175	32	256	18	62

4. What comes next?

8 2 4 8 2 16 8 128 16 –

5. The black ball moves clockwise, first to the next corner, then missing one, then two and so forth (missing an extra corner each time). The white ball moves anti-clockwise in the same way. In how many moves will they be side by side?

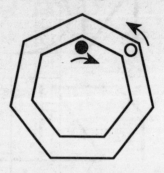

6. Which two of these shapes will form a perfect square?

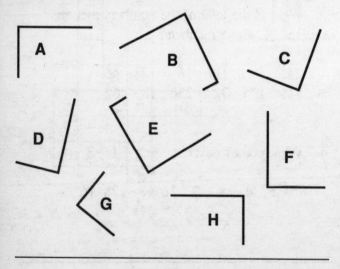

A

B

C

D

E

F

G

H

7. What is the largest total you can score in moving from A to B without moving backwards?

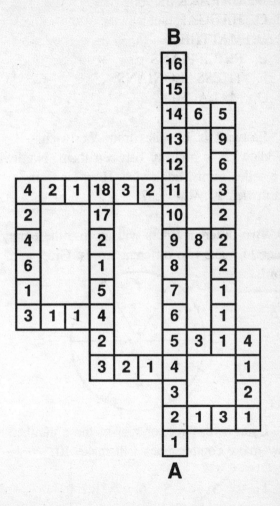

8. Which is the odd one out?
   A. ECCLESIASTES
   B. HABAKKUK
   C. HAGGAI
   D. MATTHEW
   E. PHILIPPIANS
   F. THESSALONIANS
   G. MALACHI

9. Eastwich is 12 miles from Westwich. Middlewich is midway between them. Northwich is 8 miles from Middlewich. How far from Northwich is Westwich?

10. Two different letters will go into the empty space to make two different words. Give both words.

11. Using two, three, or four of these numbers how many combinations will make 10?

   1 2 3 4 5 6 7 8 9

12. The four vanes extending from four faces of the octagon move as follows: [●] one face clockwise; [● ●] two faces anti-clockwise; [● ● ●] three faces clockwise; [● ● ● ●] four faces anti-clockwise. What will be their positions after four moves? (Choose from A, B, C or D.)

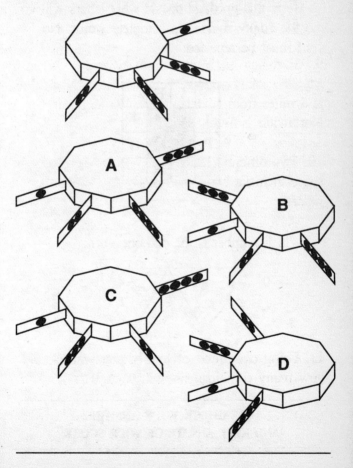

A

B

C

D

13. What have the following in common?
    A. PUP and SHEEP
    B. MOLE and FOX
    C. MOUSE and SHREW
    D. PIG and HARE

14. Copy this grid and decide what letters will go into the empty squares to complete words. No word must be repeated.

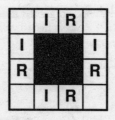

15. Which number is the odd one out?

8   9   3   6   5   4   2

Answers

1. B (Score 1 point)

2. Z (Score 1 point)

The two letters at the top make different letters when turned on their side: N becomes Z and C becomes U. The only letter at the bottom that has this characteristic is Z, which becomes N.

3. 272 (Score 1 point)

The only numbers that are squares of whole numbers are: 16 (4 squared) and 256 (16 squared).

4. 2048 (Score 1 point)

Divide the first two numbers to get the third. Multiply the next two to get the fourth. Then continue, dividing and multiplying alternately. The final number is 128 multiplied by 16 – that is, 2048.

5. Because it is a seven-sided figure they will never be side by side. After the first move they will always be two, four or six corners apart. (Score 1 point)

6. B and F (Score 1 point)

7. 151 (Score 1 point)

Either of the two possible routes on the left of the straight vertical route will give a total of 151.

8. G (Score 1 point)

All the others contain two identical consecutive letters:
A. eCClesiastes, B. habaKKuk, C. haGGai, D. maTThew, E. philiPPians, F. theSSalonians.

9. 10 miles (Score 1 point)

As X is a right-angled triangle, 100 (10 squared) is equal to 36 (6 squared) plus 64 (of which 8 is the square root). This, of course, is based on Pythagoras' theorem: 'The square on the hypotenuse is equal to the sum of the squares on the other two sides.'

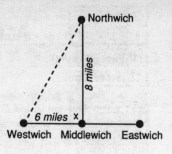

10. H and I (Score 1 point if both correct)

The words are THREAT and ATTIRE.

11. There are 9 combinations (Score 1 point if all correct)

1+9, 2+8, 3+7, 4+6, 1+2+7, 1+3+6, 1+4+5, 2+3+5, 1+2+3+4

12. B (Score 1 point)

The vanes move as follows:

 one face clockwise, finishing at '8 o'clock' approximately;

 two faces anti-clockwise, finishing at '7 o'clock';

 three faces clockwise, finishing at '10 o'clock';

 four faces anti-clockwise, finishing at '5 o'clock' approximately.

13. If the letters take a value according to their position in the alphabet, the two sides are equal. (Score 1 point)

PUP – 53, SHEEP – 53, MOLE – 45, FOX – 45, MOUSE – 73, SHREW – 73, PIG – 32 and HARE – 32.

14. (Score 1 point for any one of these)

 or alternative arrangement of the same letters

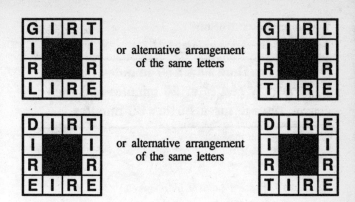

G	I	R	T
I			I
R			R
L	I	R	E

or alternative arrangement of the same letters

G	I	R	L
I			I
R			R
T	I	R	E

D	I	R	T
I			I
R			R
E	I	R	E

or alternative arrangement of the same letters

D	I	R	E
I			I
R			R
T	I	R	E

15. 4 (Score 1 point)

The only number that consists entirely of straight lines.

REMEMBER TO KEEP A NOTE OF YOUR SCORE.

Notes: You probably found this test much easier than the previous one, although the shorter time limit may have offset this advantage. Even so, you will have doubtless registered a higher score than in the previous test. Question 4 may have held you up, as did Question 5, which probably had you puzzled for a while. In Question 7 there were two routes to choose from. In Question 8 you may have been trying to decide which are in the Old Testament and which are in the New Testament, although there were some of each. Most people know Pythagoras' famous theorem, even if their knowledge of geometry is scant. Did you find THREAT elusive in Question 10, even though ATTIRE came readily to mind?

Test 3

Time limit: 50 minutes
You may rest after 20 minutes and then
resume for a further 30 minutes.

1. Where is this?

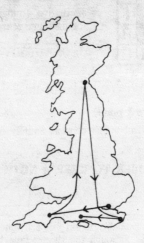

2. Many countries have changed their names in recent years. Pair the new names on the left with the old names on the right.

A. SRI LANKA   1. SIAM
B. IRAN   2. SOUTH WEST AFRICA
C. ZIMBABWE   3. KAMPUCHEA
D. NAMIBIA   4. CEYLON
E. BANGLADESH   5. RHODESIA
F. CAMBODIA   6. PERSIA
G. THAILAND   7. EAST PAKISTAN

3. What number should go into E?

2	4	2	5
3	3	3	3
DEFER	**GHILLIE**	**BURST**	**CALMNESS**
A	**B**	**C**	**D**

UNDERSTUDY
E

4. What do you make of this?

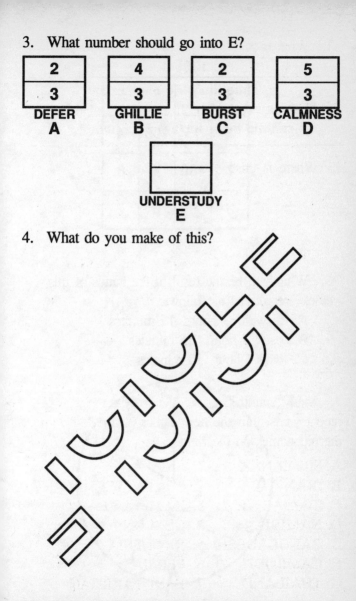

5. What is X?

3	4	6	5
2	15	105	4
7	480	X	8
8	9	6	7

6. What will be the result if the hands of this clock are moved as follows:

A. forward 3 hours, 15 minutes
B. back 4 hours, 25 minutes
C. back 1 hour, 30 minutes

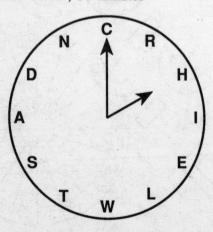

7. What is the last line?

```
A  Y  B
D  W  C
F  T  G
K  P  J
O  K  P
-  -  -
```

8. Three players each throw three darts that, starting from X, score as follows.

A. clockwise: the first three numbers divisible by 3 – all doubles;

B. anti-clockwise: the first three numbers divisible by 4 – all doubles;

C. clockwise: the first three numbers divisible by 4 – all trebles.

What did each player score?

9. Insert arithmetical signs between these numbers to justify the equation. You must give two different solutions.

1   2   3   4   5   6   7   =   3

10. Which letters below belong to A, B and C?

    A. AFHLTZ
    B. KMNVWYZ
    C. DEFHKLMN

    EGOIQUX

11. A composer is 'hidden' in each of these:

A. THE COSTA BLANCA HAS MUCH
    ATTRACTION

B. IS ALBERT AT HOME? SEE, WILL YOU?

C. HE CAME ON SATURDAY,
    UNSUSPECTED

D. TOM HAS HELPED ROBERT

12. Which is the odd one out?
    A. COTTON
    B. DOODLING
    C. DIGGING
    D. HOLLOW
    E. SUFFUSE

13. The ball in A moves clockwise, first one letter, then missing one and going onto the next, then missing two, and so on. If it lands on a consonant the ball in B moves to one number clockwise; if it lands on a vowel the ball in B moves to the third number anti-clockwise. If the ball in B lands on an even number the ball in C moves three letters clockwise; if it lands on an odd number the ball in C moves four letters anti-clockwise. What word will be spelt by the ball in C after seven moves?

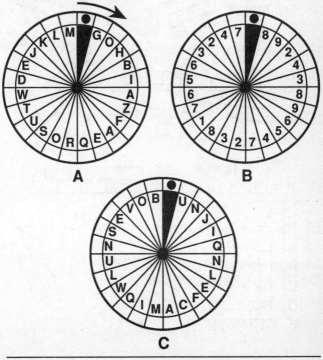

A

B

C

14. This wall has been demolished by a careless driver. Can you reconstruct it from four of the pieces below?

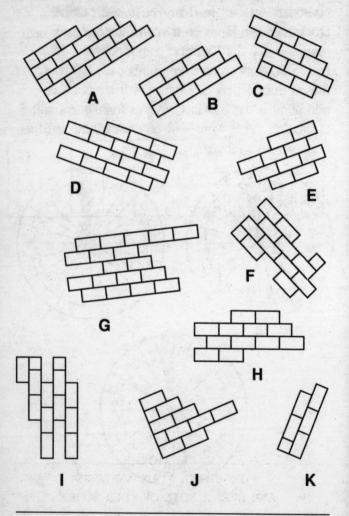

A

B

C

D

E

G

F

H

I

J

K

15. In a terrace of five houses, numbered 1, 3, 5, 7 and 9, Charles lives next door to Alf; Ernie lives next door to Bert; Alf lives next door but one to Bert; Dave lives next door but one to Charles; Charles lives at number 9. Where does each man live?

Answers

1. Leeds **(Score 1 point)**

The arrows indicate the route taken from the start (in London) to the end. Take the initials of the cities and towns passed on the journey: LONDON, EXETER, EDINBURGH, DOVER, SOUTHAMPTON.

2. A – 4, B – 6, C – 5, D – 2, E – 7, F – 3 and G – 1 **(Score 1 point if all correct)**

3.

6
4

(Score 1 point)

The lower number represents the number of alphabetically <u>consecutive</u> letters in the word. The upper number represents the number of letters remaining.

4. ICICLE **(Score 1 point)**

The word has been cut in half lengthways and the top half placed upside down below the lower half:

5. 315 **(Score 1 point)**

The number in the centre squares is the product minus the sum of the three numbers in the corner squares around it. For example, in the top left hand quarter:

3	4
2	(15)

The product of 2, 3 and 4 is 24 and the sum of 2, 3 and 4 is 9; 24 minus 9 gives 15 – as shown in the adjacent centre square.

6. CHILDREN **(Score 1 point)**

Present time indicated – CH, A. Forward to 5.15 – IL, B. Back to 12.50 – DR, C. Back to 11.20 – EN.

7. VEU (**Score 1 point**)

Zigzag from A (top left): A, C, F, J, O and (U). Zigzag from B (top right): B, D, G, K, P and (V). (First missing one letter, then two, then three and so on.) The centre vertical line (from Y) progresses in the same way downwards: Y, W, T, P, K and (E).

8. A scores 78, B scores 80, C scores 84 (**Score 1 point if all correct**)

Individual scores are: A. 36 12 30, B. 40 24 16, C. 12 48 24.

9. + + + + ÷ − +, + + + + + ÷ (**Score 1 point if both correct**)

10. A. E, B. X, C. I (**Score 1 point**)

Each letter in the first row contains horizontal strokes; each letter in the second row contains diagonal strokes; each letter in the third row contains vertical strokes.

11. A. BACH, B. BRAHMS, C. STRAUSS, D. MAHLER (**Score 1 point if all correct**)

You will doubtless already be familiar with sentences that contain 'hidden' words. Thus, in this sentence is 'hidden' the word **sonata**: 'A per<u>son at a</u> meeting.' In this problem there are 'hidden' names, *except that they appear in alternate letters!* For example, in A. THE COSTA <u>BLANCA</u> <u>H</u>AS MUCH ATTRACTION.

12. B (**Score 1 point**)

All the others contain two identical consonants surrounded by two identical vowels: A. cOTTOn, C. dIGGIng, D. hOLLOw, E. sUFFUse. B contains two identical vowels surrounded by two identical consonants: DOODling.

13. JONQUIL (**Score 1 point**)

The moves result as follows:

	Ball A	Ball B	Ball C
1st move	G	8	J
2nd move	H	9	O
3rd move	A	4	N
4th move	E	6	Q
5th move	U	7	U
6th move	K	6	I
7th move	I	8	L

14. A, B, J and K
(Score 1 point if all correct)

They fit together like this:

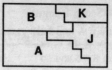

15. 1 Emie, 3 Bert, 5 Dave, 7 Alf, 9 Charles (Score 1 point if all correct)

REMEMBER TO KEEP A NOTE OF YOUR SCORE

Notes: Question 1 called for some elementary knowledge of British geography. These problems are not too difficult on the whole, although Questions 8 and 13 may have taken a while to work out. In Question 11 the *alternate* 'hidden' letters may have foxed you. Question 14 was very difficult without the aid of tracing paper – you had to rely solely on your eye and your imagination!

NOW TOTAL ALL YOUR SCORES FOR THE
THREE TESTS IN THIS SECTION AND CHECK
YOUR RATING WITH THE FOLLOWING
SECTION, AFTER WHICH YOU CAN FIND
YOUR RATING FOR ALL THE TESTS.

Ratings in Group III

Test 1 – average 6 points
Test 2 – average 9 points
Test 3 – average 7 points

Out of a possible 45
Over 32 Excellent
29 – 32 Very good
23 – 28 Good
22 Average
20-21 Fair
Under 20 Poor

Now work out your total score for all the tests and find your rating from the next page.

Overall Ratings for all the Tests

The total number of possible points is 173, and the average score throughout is 81: Group I – 28, Group II – 31, Group III – 22, Total – 81.

Over 108	Excellent
96 – 107	Very good
82 – 95	Good
81	Average
70 – 80	Fair
Under 70	Poor

I hope you enjoyed pitting your wits against these problems, and I freely admit that many of them were extremely difficult. Yet I have always been fascinated by the fact that a problem that may have one person completely baffled can be solved almost immediately by another. Proof has been provided over and over again that some people have a flair for numbers – and consequently do well in numerical problems – while others show a distinct preference for verbal questions. Honours are fairly even as far as spatial discrimination is concerned because, irrespective of personal predilection, solutions either came readily or – unfortunately – not at all.

But, reverting to my introductory notes, a high rating may give you justifiable reason for self-congratulation, but a low score should not make you feel you are a failure in the intellectual stakes. The problems have been devised from beginning to end with a view to affording diversion more than proving or disproving the presence of 'intelligence'.